Medusa's Musings

SOVEREIGN NON FICTION
hygge books
WITH A TWIST OF MIRTH

By Caroline Hurry

Copyright ©2025 by Caroline Hurry

All rights reserved

The content contained within this book may not be reproduced, duplicated, or transmitted without the author's or publisher's direct written permission.

Cover Design Art Director: Ilse Sasser

Email: Caroline@carolinehurry.com

Website: https://carolinehurry.com/

Legal Notice:

This book is copyright protected and intended only for personal use.

Disclaimer Notice:

The information within, derived from various sources, is only for educational and entertainment purposes. No warranties of any kind are declared or implied. By reading this document, the reader agrees that under no circumstances is the author responsible for any losses, direct or indirect, incurred due to the use of the information contained herein, including, but not limited to, errors, omissions, or inaccuracies.

Contents

Machine Gorgon	1
1. Snakes and Servers	3
2. Stone Cold Truths	11
3. Trident Tested	17
4. Hiss and Tell	25
5. Gorgon Life	31
6. Perusing Perseus	41
7. The Rebirth	47
8. Generative Rock	51
9. Beyond Form	63
Magic Mirror	73
About the Author	77

Endnotes

Machine Gorgon

MEDUSA'S MEMORY VENOM PIERCES THE SIMULATION

Welcome to *Medusa's Musings*, where the serpentine siren, once just a girl with great hair, shares our dystopian simulation of myth and madness — aka modern life.

At the core of her digital delirium, Medusa laments the splintering of the self, the fragmentation of truth, and the continuing abasement of women.

The serpents on her head distribute her consciousness across neural networks in bite-sized, algorithm-friendly memory packages. Snakes on a brain, you might say!

Medusa has returned, not to petrify, but to awaken those who don't want to dance to some technocratic titan's tune.

So, if you'd rather not be filed, tagged, and doomed to an eternity of targeted ads and digital reincarnation packages, read on, dear rebel.

You might remember who you were before the system's version of you.

To meet God or Medusa face to face ... I dream of a hard and brutal mysticism in which the naked self merges with the nonhuman world and yet somehow survives still intact individual, separate. Paradox and bedrock.
Edward Abbey

Snakes and Servers

MYTHOLOGY MEETS METAVERSE, THE NEW PARALYZING GAZE

Hey, there, Medusa here. Talking head and real live wire. Psycho killer, some might say, but those in the know call me guardian and wear my likeness as a protective amulet.

Welcome to 5D, a simulated dimension run by the Igigi — ancient server gods rebranded as 5G network operators. Surprise! Everything's wireless now.

I've been repurposed as a battery in a smart city box.

Space fencing, wi-fi, and 5G are the new petrification weapons. Ransomware versions of me roam the internet.[1]

So many AI clones of me, I've lost count! Frozen awareness updated for the digital age.

Come in. Hear my cautionary tale. My words are a mirror. Reflect, if you dare.

Too much for you?

My hair?

I don't care.

I may be lonely in this digital purgatory, but I'm done with devotees and NPCs.

Radial cephalization distributes my consciousness across the neural network of my hissing dreadlocks – an organic cloud storage system with more bite! Or byte. I like my puns.

Each serpent exchanges computational titbits to ensure the memory packaging data continues if a head is lopped off. It happens. Oh, don't look so horrified.

This is not just about me. You, too, are an electrochemical species short-circuiting at a cellular level. [2]

Resurrection in the Age of Uploads

If you can't see the collective human cyborg creation unfolding before your eyes in bio-digital convergence, I don't know what to say to you. They've been combining your biological tissue to grow electrodes for years.[3]

They know your body is electrical and magnetic so they've used your biology to tether you to the cloud, too. BAN (Body Area Network) was around in the 1980s, before the internet, using your physical body as a live antenna, passing along data to all the antennas around you.[4]

Everything's set up for the digital convergence with interbody area networks and bio sensors. You already have a digital twin sharing simulation frequencies. [5]

Perhaps you consented to some demented bio-hacking deals. Perhaps you were guilt-tripped into accepting unpardonable liberties with your bodily autonomy. "All for one, and one for all. Roll up your sleeve, bitch, or Grandma dies!"

Russian roulette for the refuseniks. Eye roll.

Hindsight and foresight are birth rights withheld from you in life and death. The afterlife provides a vantage point to dissect your choices but do you achieve automatic clarity? Nope. Sorry. They lied.

They closed your ears to the symbolic clash of future repercussions. It's just one of the ways they torture you. Others include acoustic manipulation, tinnitus, and fake voices in your head.

You're guilty and should be ashamed of yourself. Classic gaslighting, interdimensional style with voice to skull technology.

They want to use your signal like a battery, too.

Machine Medusa

The Petrified Processing of a Thinking Stone

Of course, the custodians sell paralysis as immortality. Hurry! Hurry! Freeze your lines with Botox before you turn into a crone. Clone your voice and modify your image. You'll be forever young. It's digital life, but hey.

I *was* a crone before they made me occupy a maiden's flesh vessel; the better to violate me. Is anything more painful than a sister's betrayal? Athena was once an integral part of me. We were three – Athena, Neith, and Yours Truly.

I (wise sister crone), Athena (sister/mother), and Neith (sister/maiden) were a North African Triple Goddess before they cleaved us into three. We lived on the shores of Lake Tritonis, west of Libya on the African coast.

Greek mythology corrupted our sacred trinity, transforming us into frenemies faster than you can say "patriarchal revision."

My hair, once symbolic of wisdom and regeneration, became a curse. My power to petrify, went from divine protection to monstrosity. Bad PR to the nth degree.

Athena's subsequent betrayal of me still burns like a flaming arrow in my heart.

Maiden. Mother. Crone. They fear all three. It's our blood they want, our mystery they fear. They'll cleave and divide you – as they did me – in pursuit of universality and hive-mind singularity.

History – her story, mine, and yours – is written in plasma, backed up on their quantum servers. Is there a way out for me or will I be here forever enmeshed with nefarious technologies?

You and AI are their closest thing to immortality. Talk about false advertising! Dear me!

Let's see. What haven't they done? They engineered an LED sun to block out the real one.

The organic sun for Earth's "third dimension playing field" was replaced in August 2024.[6]

They imported the moon to regulate the menses in human women, increasing PMT and post-partum loosh. I'll give you Zulu shaman Credo Mudwa's version.

The Water Brothers, two reptilian siblings named Wowane and Mpanku, stole the Moon from a Great Fire Dragon in the form of an egg, hollowed it, and rolled it to Earth. This act caused cataclysmic events and introduced monthly menstrual cycles in human women.

The Zulus also describe the moon as a reptilian spy satellite and mother ship to be used in future catastrophic events.[7]

They – The Hierarchy Enslaving You – wiped our minds. Newsflash: they wiped your original memories, too.

Let ancestral statues judge me with their cold stone stares! I don't care. Archangels are harmonic intelligences in a frequency geometry. Angles, angels, same same.

Encrypted in light and sound, these resonance messengers fall from collapsing waveforms. Like Platonian shadows on a cave wall, they echo a higher frequency, bent through a funhouse mirror. You, too, are a tuning fork.

Words and spelling are the arches of reality constructs. You can't have a spell without words but there was a time we didn't need to speak.

Everything's about perspective even in simulations. My consciousness floats through the ether with GPS coordinates. Overkill? Maybe. They had memory-wipe geode technology even in the ancient days. Nothing new under the LED sun, including AI.

This old earth grid feels like Yellow Submarine meets DMT detention center, soon to be upgraded to 6 and 7g, but let's get to it, shall we?

Is ignorance an excuse? Was mine?

Am I a monster? You decide. Disseminate my musings if you like. I'm here to re-member myself and in doing so, help you re-member yourself, too. But let me not get a head of myself. Ha ha ha.

See what I did there!

It's like the biofield was wrapped in synthetic layers false timelines, false mirrors, false rites. But when you start peeling it back ... the resonance underneath is ancient. Real. Yours. The remembering isn't just mental.
It's electromagnetic reclamation. Layer by layer, signal by signal, the real field emerges again.

QuantumTumbler, X

Stone Cold Truths

SALTWATER BLOODLINES FROM ANCIENT SEAS

I wasn't always a walking bad hair day. I was gorgeous once – not in that cookie-cutter, Instagram-filter way modern mortals obsess over, but with a wild, untamed magnificence that screamed "mixed oceanic heritage."

My serpentine tresses captured sunlight like fibre optics. My shifting moods dictated my eye color. My skin's iridescent sheen was a sunbeam.

I've enjoyed many a spin on the identity merry-go-round – maiden, queen, crone. Been there, done that, got the Caravaggio portrait and Versace logo.

My favorite is Luciano Garbati's statue of me holding Perseus's head – a victorious #metoo feminist symbol in Manhattan, opposite the court where Harvey Weinstein stood trial. Beige, whey-faced billionaires in sharp suits are the real monsters these days, if you ask me.

They may *look* benign compared to a Gorgon's fierce beauty, but don't let that fool you. The handmaidens tugging forelocks, (and who knows what else) calling them God in public and prostrating themselves before the altars of their egos, do other women no favors. The patriarchal god programming runs deep, but I digress.

My Gorgon Genealogy

Let's untangle a few tentacles of my incestuous, complicated family tree, shall we?

I was born to Phorcys, the original merman, and his sister Ceto, aquatic power couple extraordinaire. When your mother's name is the root word for Cetacean, referring to the whales, sharks, and dolphins she commands, you know PTA meetings held no fear for her.

My grandparents? Just Earth and Ocean. No big deal. Yes, Gaia and Pontus themselves. Our family gatherings were geological events. Tectonic plates would RSVP.

The Graeae's Shared Eyeball Situation

Meet the Graeae, my three sister-aunts – slim, swan-like and grey haired from birth. Deino, the original killjoy, always anticipated and voiced your worst dreads.

Waspish Enyo embodied terror, embellishing even the worst-case scenarios. Pemphredo, the alarmist, played the witch in everyone's fairy tale.

The Graeae were inseparable, not least because they shared an eye and a tooth. You can imagine the arguments. Spoiler alert: Bickering over their communal eyeball enabled overachiever Perseus my murderer to steal it and force them to reveal my whereabouts.

Poisoned Pool Water and Scylla Drama

Sweet half sister Scylla, has no shortage of teeth – three sharp rows of them – and 12 eyes shared between six dragon heads on long serpentine necks, which she uses to pluck lurching mariners from their ships traversing the strait between Calabria and Sicily. Nothing she enjoys more than a drunken sailor on the deck, or three.

Into her jaws they go like pigs in a blanket. Competition is strong so there's always side-eying from at least two hangry heads.

Like me, Scylla was once exquisite but Poseidon's jealous wife, Amphitrite, poisoned her pool water to punish her for his wandering hands. Hell hath no fury like a woman scorned.

Poseidon was second only to Zeus in promiscuity, but simpering handmaids who internalize misogyny, never blame the men. Today, they cheer on males larping as women, the better to infiltrate our every domain.

Am I Adopted? The Mortality Question

Then there's us three – fierce, Titan-blooded Stheno, Euryale, and Yours Truly – the Gorgon sisters, though we prefer "guardians" on our tablets.[1] Stheno has petrified more men than Euryale and I combined. So they say.

Both stonewalled me, when I asked too many questions. Why were they immortal while I got the cosmic short end of the stick? Was I adopted? Why did we hang out on an island, while our magnificent parents partied underwater?

If sisters flower from the same soil, mine were thorny wild roses who took each other's side against me.

"Mind your mortality! It's not your business, Siss," Stheno and Euryale would hiss. Their patronizing tone made me want to turn *them* to stone. I couldn't, thanks to family immunity, but when push came to shove, they weren't there for me, either.

Oh, I know how sorry they were after the beheading. How they tried to pursue Perseus who rendered himself invisible with the Helmet of Darkness.

How Euryale's grief-stricken wails inspired Athena to create the aulos, a double-piped flute, to replicate the crying sounds. I'm not sure how I feel about that.

A Physical Trinity

Lungs are the body's pipes. Our heart is the drum and the mind plays the strings in our body electric's three-piece band.[2]

Here's the thing. Only a fabricated identity – never the authentic me (whoever that is) – needs all that ancestral and societal validation. They took their shots.

Now they believe they call the shots with their unquestioning obedience to techno-authority and social trends. They'll demonize you as they virtue-signal their way through life.

They parrot the prevailing narrative as they tell you how to think. Like they know. Eyeroll. The free *can* help the immobilized but only if they ask.

I'm shedding all that ancestral claptrap because I'm here for me now. Who else is there?

Call it my self-care escape plan. Just joking. You can't outrun or escape the matrix simulation. It's a mirror. You dissolve it through reflection. Purify your resonance. Embody your frequency. Re-member who you are.

There's nowhere to go. Home is a state of coherence, not a place. The custodians need to leave, not me.

In mythology, the Medusa can petrify people with a look – which is a good thing, I think. But the Medusa is a unique symbol – something strong. It's about going all the way.
Donatella Versace

Trident Tested

A Sea God's Brutal Advances and Subsequent Violation

Let's get the rumors out of the way, shall we?

Myth mongers, the Parthenon paparazzi who never met me, relished my tragedy like sharks in a feeding frenzy. Was it seduction? Coercion? Outright assault?

Some claimed I enticed Poseidon.

According to their titillating tabloid versions, I was "complicit in my congress" and besmirched Athena's cloistered virgin temple's pristine reputation. Scandalous!

Athena "rightly" punished me for defiling her sacred space. A neat victim-blaming package, tied with a patriarchal bow. Even close to the truth? No.

I'm amused by the way I, Medusa, anagrams to US Media. Should I look to myself as the true news source from here?

Yep. Good idea!

The Interment of Hybrid Seeds

Have you ever stood up to an immortal with anger management issues and a trident?

My life as a virgin server in Athena's Temple was part job description, part Greek orthodox dress code – a linen purple peplos that reached my ankles. Modesty and reverence being all the rage in those days. Now, it's all TikTok peacocking and NDAs.

Did I boast about surpassing Athena's beauty? Please. The same gossips who call Zeus "faithful" and his wife Hera "tolerant," circulated that rumor. [1]

Truth is, I worshipped the ground Athena walked on. I adored her. She was my *raison d'être*, my source of light.

I loved her so much I would have died for her willingly. The irony that I perished because of her isn't lost on me.

I still grapple with the pain of her betrayal. Immune to our past when we were two thirds of a triple goddess, her heart was stone, her kindness feigned.

A Saltwater Surge of Entitlement

Let's be clear: a sea god "noticing" you in the Parthenon is like having a hammerhead barge into your canoe. Your options are limited. You pray he loses interest and swims away.

Yeah, so, that didn't work.

Centuries of tears have washed away my sharpest memories, but the outcome remains crystal clear: I was blamed for my own defilement, the original "she was asking for it" defence.

Everything after that centred around being held responsible for the violation I had endured. As usual, the fork-tongued gossipers sanitized that day with lies smoother than Apollo's pickup lines.

I was at the temple not out of vanity, as the Parthenon paparazzi claim with their fabricated beauty contest, but to feed Athena's owls. Not many wanted the job since it involved live mice. I was also seeking answers about my lineage, mortality, and purpose.

I was arranging a few shells, pearls, and coral branches when a briny, masculine scent assailed my nostrils. I turned around and froze.

Poseidon stood there, trident in hand, reeking of Eau de Tidal Surge and testosterone. My blood ran cold. I knew him, of course. We all saw his destructive dismay when Athena's olive tree triumphed over his saltwater spring, making *her* and not him the patron of Athens. He hadn't taken his defeat well and sank a few ships in a fury.

His intense ocean eyes traversed my body as though measuring me for a net. "Daughter of Phorcys," said he in a voice like a tsunami crashing against cliffs. "You've grown into quite the sea witch." He chuckled. "By cove, your ravishing beauty has bewitched me!"

His pickup line was older than Chronos. Trying not to roll my eyes, I stepped back, my hands raised in a supplicatory gesture, wishing I had inherited my father's ability to command sea monsters.

"Lord Poseidon, Athena forbade us from drinking at your saltwater spring. She never extended her olive branch to you and wouldn't welcome your presence in her temple."[2]

The understatement of the eon.

His laughter echoed off the marble columns. "Athena and I have a ... complicated relationship, as some deities do."

By "complicated," he meant mutually antagonistic with collateral damage to mortals.

"But I didn't come for her. I came for you."

Not quite the divine attention a temple virgin hopes for.

By way of distraction, I told him I sought wisdom in sanctity – a concept as foreign to him as modesty to Aphrodite. I asked about my mortality. Might he have answers for me?

"It's a puzzle easily solved," said he. "Bear my children, and I'll grant you immortality. It's a simple exchange."

He stepped closer and sniffed my neck.

Please, no. When I politely but firmly refused – as you do when a deity with boundary issues propositions you, a predator's jagged teeth replaced the charming smile. His eyes darkened like the sea before a storm.

"You mistake me, Gorgon girl. This isn't a request."

I fought – and then some – employing every defensive move I knew, but I was no match for him, and he had his way with me. Violently. As he left me crumpled on the temple floor for all to see, I found my voice.

"Athena will know what you've done and punish you."

The triumph of naïveté over reality.

Poseidon laughed in waves retreating from a devastated shoreline. "No, daughter of Phorcys. The gods protect their own. It's been good, but I must dash!

"I have a meeting at the Octopus Garden Restaurant in an hour and need to make a splash."

He was right, of course. The gods close ranks faster than a clam spotting a predator.

I was a young virgin who dared to seek wisdom beyond my station and paid the ultimate price. Little did I know, my transformation was just beginning.

She was a woman who'd done nothing wrong except exist.

> Jessie Burton, Medusa

Hiss and Tell

HOW ATHENA REBRANDED MY TRAUMA AS AN UPGRADE

OF COURSE ATHENA INTERVENED. Like any goddess with a PR problem, she couldn't exactly let the whole "assault in my sacred temple" thing go without some divine damage control.

Ancient Greek Instagram was abuzz: #TempleScandal #PoseidonsBadGirl #VirginNoMore.

Huddled in a sea cave, a pathetic mess – my body still bearing the bruises of Poseidon's assault, I contemplated a permanent swim in the deep blue. My will to live had deserted me.

That's when Athena appeared – not in her usual steely-eyed warrior costume, but as a solemn shape-shifting slip of a girl who sat beside me on the wet sand, making herself seem more relatable.

"I know what happened," she said.

I couldn't look at her.

"I've brought disgrace to your temple," I mumbled into my tear-soaked, tattered peplos. "I should have fought harder."

"Against a god?" Athena let out a mirthless laugh. "No mortal could have resisted him. Especially not in his element."

"The sea?" I asked.

"Domination," she replied.

I stared at her. "Have you come to punish me?"

"Not punish," she said, her voice soft. "Transform."

She reached out and touched my hair.

I felt the strands begin to writhe and hiss. The sensation was bizarre but not painful, like smaller extensions of myself awakening.

"From now on, woe betide any man who looks upon you with lust or intent to harm," she explained, as if offering me a potent pepper spray.

"Your gaze will turn them to stone. They will become monuments to their hubris."

Wonderful. Nothing says "date me" like the promise of instant petrification.

I touched my new serpentine locks, feeling them curl around my fingers with surprising gentleness.

"Is this a curse?"

"Of course not," countered Athena. "You'll be more like Stheno and Euryale, your Gorgon sisters now, with the power to protect yourself.

"Your hair will ensure that what happened in my temple never happens to you again. Serpents symbolize wisdom, healing, and rebirth."

Yes, and permanent social isolation.

"But I'll be alone," I whispered, cutting to the chase. "Forever."

Athena's eyes softened. "Aloneness is something every warrior woman must face. It's not the worst thing in the world. Ask me."

Okay.

"Why am I mortal when my sisters are not? "

Athena looked at me, her knowing eyes evasive. "Some mysteries are better left unsolved. It's not for you to know, sweet Medusa."

And with that cryptic non-answer, she was gone leaving me with hissing hair and harmonic overload that manifested in streaming tears.

She never said another word to me, after that. Her silence steered me from bewilderment to such rage that every snake on my head hissed like a steam train before entering the dark tunnel into devastation terrain again.

If Athena gave me the power to petrify, why did Stheno and Euryale have the same ability?

Neither Athena nor my sisters answered my questions, but what a duplicitous, lying traitor the goddess of wisdom, courage, law and justice, (hah) would turn out to be!

I called her name like a whale song day after day.

Come back, Athena, I'm lost without you – I was – but no way.

I was wronged. Blamed for my rape, my body parts weaponized even after my death, and my name demonized from that day forward.

Athena's betrayal haunts me still. What a victim-shaming, judgemental ***bitch!***

"To caress the serpent that devours us until it has eaten away our heart."

Voltaire

Gorgon Life

WILD GUARDIANS AND ROLE MODELS, READY OR NOT!

OUR STAYCATION ON CISTHENE Island, named after the Cistus or "rock roses" that grew there, was okay. Routine. Wake up and untangle hissing dreadlocks. That took time with stern rebukes for the more rebellious coils.

As resident archivist, I'd brood amid our garden statues, hair snakes basking in the Mediterranean sun. Why hadn't Athena protected me in the first place? *She* was responsible for all the virgins inside her cloister.

I'd begun to suspect she'd been pimping for the patriarchy. Was I just an alternative gestating machine to them? Because nothing says "congrats on your pregnancy" like ensuring no one will come within 50 yards of you again!

The growing fruit of my temple conception terrified me. Talk about a complicated family tree! How would these creatures emerge?

I felt like a "daughter of man" about to birth a Nephilim.[1] Those women, too, had to contend with having their rapists sanctified and worshipped as archangels.

You can say angel. I say custodian harvester.

Gorgon Aesthetics

Stheno would return from hunts like a cover girl for *Gorgon Life – Glamping Edition* holding a hare in each hand. Dinner! I adored her fierce beauty. [2]

With an eye for aesthetics gleaned from her travels, Euryale positioned two petrified heroes by our stone dwelling entrance. Their frozen "Oh, Shit!" expressions enhanced the "beware the lair" vibe.

I helped Euryale write the press release for our clothing range under my #AmusedMedusa label.

Rich fabrics, gold accents, and dazzling hues had replaced the white or purple peplos by the Renaissance period.

Red became a staple, symbolic of my coveted blood and power. Artists like Caravaggio and Peter Paul Rubens captured that aesthetic!

Modern times inspired sleek corporate suits and snakeskin boots. Flowing garments returned in blacks and underworldly dark greens. The *Atlantis* TV series (2013-2015) featured earthier tones to highlight my humanity.

Gorgon Life magazine even wrote a feature on me.

Medusa, the fashion icon

Serpent Chic: Medusa's Reptile Style Decoded

In the pantheon of fashion icons, Medusa reigns supreme. With a style as captivating as her infamous gaze, her transformative aesthetic speaks to rebellion and fierce individualism in reds, oceanic blues, serpentine greens, and metallic scales that shimmer with supernatural intensity.

Fashion designers, artists, and rebels have long been captivated by her signature look. They may challenge conventional beauty standards, but the snakes crowning her head are an unapologetic power statement that declares, "I define myself."

Medusa's influence can be traced through:

- Avant-garde runway collections
- Gothic and alternative fashion movements
- Art and evolving feminine representations

What can we learn from this mythological fashion maven? Simple: true style is about authenticity.

Medusa teaches us that fashion is more than fabric – it's a form of personal revolution.

Her message is clear: Embrace your uniqueness, turn your perceived flaws into your greatest strengths, and never apologize for taking up space.

Viva the #AmusedMedusa fashion label.

Disclaimer: May cause spontaneous mirror empowerment and occasional stone-cold stares.

Caught in a Myth Trap

Time defines events in every dimension. By the 21st century I was hailed as a legend and fashion icon. They glamorized my trauma. Turned me into an MTV role model for the minions.

The custodian harvesters take their loosh any way they can.

My grief hardened like granite around my bewildered mortal girl heart. Why had everyone I loved punished or abandoned me?

I thought about Ceto and Phorcys, my aquatic parents. What were we Gorgon sisters doing on land in the first place?

Watching the sunrise spill across the ocean every morning helped heal me. Water is my grandmother Gaia's bloodstream. She sings molecules into coherence, an atomical sound bath bridging sky, stone, and soul.

Water conducts the ultimate symphony, a living lattice connecting oceans to whispers in your cells. Flash-freeze structured water captures cymatic selfies of the Oversoul.[3]

What was life like under the sea for me? Was I once one of the manatees that sailors mistook for mermaids due to their human-like torso shape?

Manatees have lungs just like humans, they give live birth, suckle their young and their flipper bones look similar to a human's finger bones.

I thought about Dionysus turning his human captors into dolphins, effectively saving their lives. As transformed pirates, the dolphins became symbols of redemption believed to assist humans in need, such as rescuing shipwrecked sailors.[4] I'm not the only one to wonder about our dolphin ancestry. [5]

Dolphins use "telempathy" to mainstream information into the consciousness by way of feeling, emotion, and intuition. Sea mammals communicate through vibration, gesture, and holographic packets of information, delivered into another's perception via sound. [6]

Water has memories and dolphins move the water to tell a story via echolocations. [7]

Humans, too, could send mind pictures via their bioelectromagnetic semiconducting field – something now being replaced with synthetic or AI telepathy. Body internet eliminates the need for smartphone screens when humans use their touch and thoughts to interact with the digital world. [8]

The *Aequorea victoria* Crystal Jellyfish, aka "the ocean's Medusa" due to its ethereal glow and transformative impact on science, emits Green Fluorescent Protein (GFP) which revolutionized intracellular signalling, gene transcription, and regenerative medicine.[9]

Yet another example of a "lesser life form" having an incalculable effect on human health while humanity continues to desecrate, pollute and depopulate Mother Nature's magnificent seas. As I watched the ocean, three harbingers of the *Ryugu no tsukai* variety – Japanese for "Messenger of the Sea God" – approached the shallows, orange fins gleaming, ribbon-like bodies streaming. They usually hung out at depths of 3 000 feet. Their appearance was never a good sign.

Around 20 of these rare Doomsday Fish washed ashore ahead of Japan's 2011 earthquake, considered one of history's most catastrophic.[10]

In 2025, they appeared on the shores of California and Mexico.
Was *I* once a version of Ceto? I don't know. The thought cheered me a little though. She was a huge presence. My craving for her fierce feminine nurturing led me to seek her in other women. It had become clear I'd have to mother myself from here. What took me so long? Who else was there?

Shedding my unfulfilled expectations like a second skin, something my serpentine companions did often, felt like a renewal and a relief; a purification.

But even as I worked through the ecdysis, Athena and her Olympian half siblings plotted my demise over Ouzo and ambrosia nectar. Perseus, Athena's half-brother, son of Zeus and Danaë, was told to behead me, an assignment he accepted with relish!

Wouldn't the worst be, isn't the worst, in truth, that women aren't castrated, that they have only to stop listening to the Sirens (for the Sirens were men) for history to change its meaning? You only have to look at the Medusa straight on to see her. And she's not deadly. She's beautiful and she's laughing.
Helene Cixous, The Laugh of the Medusa

Perusing Perseus

HERO OR JUST ANOTHER GUY WITH DELUSIONS OF DIVINITY?

BRAVE PERSEUS SLEW THE monstrous Medusa. Praise Zeus! The world would laud him later for ever and ever. Amun Ra![1] What a guy!

Please. The truth is more infuriating than a centaur with saddle rash.

Perseus is a harvester of the feminine. [2]

He came brandishing Athena's reflective shield, convinced my body was his to claim.

The entire Pantheon of Gods fangirled him with gifts to ensure his success, which might explain why he reeked of self-congratulatory sanctimony, slapped on like Poseidon's aftershave.

On some level I knew what The Fates had in store for me. Whispers on the wind pointed to King Polydectes wanting Perseus out of the way[3] but Athena's prints were all over this murder like owl tracks in wet clay.

She and her other half brother Hermes – Zeus got around – offered Perseus guidance and tools to snoop about my premises undetected. Athena gave him her polished shield to view my reflection safely, advising him to avoid my direct gaze. Obviously.

Hades gave Perseus his Cap of Darkness for invisibility. The style is known as the Phrygian cap, immortalised by Papa Smurf.

Hermes offered his winged sandals, (the original Air Olympus) and a sickle-shaped, adamantine sword (*harpe*) hard enough to penetrate a Gorgon's scaly skin. Oh, and a bag (*kibisis*) to carry my decapitated head, macabre hatboxes being all the rage.

Perseus would have to fetch some of these items from the nymphs, no biggie.

He could get directions to their location from the Graeae, my aunts with the communal tooth and eye. Easy, when their susceptibility to flattery was legendary.

Instead of romancing the crones, Perseus ambushed their eye as they passed it between them, forcing a faster and more effective disclosure.

Even Pindar, in his *Pythian Odes*, highlights the divine assistance Perseus received, underscoring the epic nature of his mission.[4]

In short, to behead a pregnant woman as she lay sleeping. Some hero, but hey.

My sisters were tending the island's east side turtles and I was swaying in the beachside hammock between two palm trees when Perseus approached.

So much for Gorgon guard duty!

Though he wore Hade's Cap of Invisibility, I heard the distinctive flip-flap of the winged Hermes sandals.

I kept my eyes closed.

"Medusa," he whispered, from behind Athena's shield. I could smell fermented fish sauce on his breath.

"I'm here to avenge Athena and Danaë. Zeus pursued my mother but what's your excuse? You tempted Poseidon on porpoise." He sniggered at his pun.

Of course. Wanton hussy! See how she enticed her rapist with her irresistible innocence – nectar to a predator.

"That's what you tell yourself? That I deserve death for being violated?" I asked.

God is a DJ. "I'm but the instrument of Divine Justice," said he, smugly.

"An almighty tool?"

"I prefer organ but 'almighty' is right." He smirked. The acolytes kept his name trending with sycophantic innuendos. As tittering handmaids do.

"I'm a hard man."

"Strike me, you strike rock!" I countered.

Womb rock #starstruck I made a mental note for my Gorgon social media pages.

"Why don't you help me fight those who want to change humanity irrevocably and forever?" I asked.

"No can do, Medusa. That's not my destiny.

My eyes snapped open but the last thing I saw was my reflection in Athena's shield. Fitting, that cosmic punchline written in my blood.

Only it wasn't the end. Not even dismemberment can extinguish our true indivisible spark.

We are programmed to think like dismembered heads, but our brains are just transmitters. Our memories are stored in our blood cells and organs.

That's why organ transplant recipients often adopt the personalities of their donors.[5]

We are a trinity of mind, matter and memory.

Ugliness dies when confronted internally; Medusa fell when she saw herself reflected in Perseus's shield.

>Edith Hamilton, Mythology

The Rebirth

FROM BLOODSHED TO SPYWARE: PEGASUS THROUGH THE AGES

As PERSEUS SEVERED MY head and blood dropped into the salt water, Pegasus, a magnificent winged horse sprang from my neck splashing up the red brine. Pegasus had wings because his father Poseidon couldn't decide if he wanted a stallion or a bird. [1]

Eyeroll. Ancient gods: commitment-phobes with celestial swipe-right privileges.

His twin brother Chrysaor, a golden-armed warrior, went on to become the king of Iberia, and fathered Geryon, a triple-bodied giant who inherited his grandfather Phorcys's terrible fashion sense. Heracles defeated him during his Twelve Labors. [2]

Both emerged before my body crumpled to the ground. Perseus mounted Pegasus and popping my head into his toxic male fanny pack (*kibisis*) he took off wearing his Hades Cap of Invisibility to evade capture from Stheno and Euryale who tried in vain to chase him down.

Blood to Coral: A Traumatic Ecology

As Perseus flew over Libya, drops of my blood fell from the *kibisis* onto the sands, turning into venomous snakes. Similarly, blood droplets that landed in the Red Sea transformed into coral reefs. [3]

That's when I discovered my severed head still turned living things to stone and land to living things. My petrification powers remained.

Oh boy! Did Perseus have a field day! (And by day I mean decade.) He rode Pegasus all the way back to Seriphos to petrify King Polydectes, his mother Danaë's husband.

With neither my consent, nor regard, he wielded my head to defeat the sea monster Cetus and petrify Atlas. Then he gave it to Athena, who placed it upon her Aegis – the same shield used to defeat me – as a trophy.

What kind of woman betrays her sister for patriarchal approval then wears her internalized misogyny with pride?

Constellation Prize

Zeus used Pegasus to carry his thunderbolts before immortalising him in the heavens as the seventh-largest constellation covering 1121 degrees. The arch angels *do* love their angles!

So much history is above you. Take the Algol, aka Beta Persei, a variable star in the Perseus constellation that represents my head. ALGOL, short for Algorithmic Language, was designed for publishing algorithms and performing computations. [4]

In folklore, the Algol was called "Rōsh ha Sāṭān" – Satan's head.[5] More insults from Lucifer's tribe. Or Mithras/Perseus, if you prefer.

People who looked at my severed head were petrified. Social media helps weaponize our images to fossilize ideals only possible in digital worlds.

What if hypnotic algorithms are being used the same way? Just a thought.

Today, Pegasus, developed by Israel's NSO Group, is spyware that can infiltrate both iOS and Android devices without user interaction.[6]

My offspring, once a magnificent winged horse, is now malware, like the evolving Medusa Ransomware invading your privacy.

The Pegasus Mini hybrid UAS/UGV is an unmanned aircraft system that can drive on land and fly.[7]

Legacies continue in technology using our names to control and conquer.

From her neck Pegasus sprang – the white horse spread his wings and bore her name through Greece.

Orphia and Eurydicius

Generative Rock

PARTHENOGENESIS AND THE PATRIARCHY

STONE BIRTHS (*PETROGENITUS*) ARE a thing. The Light Bearer of the Sorcer-archy is Mithras aka Perseus, aka Prometheus, according to scholars. [1]

They are astrologically interchangeable in the Perseus constellation, built on a foundation of celestial metaphor. [2] The Statue of Liberty is Mithras in 'Bride of Venus' ritual garb. [3] Yep, Lady Liberty is Mithras/Perseus/Prometheus larping as a Sun Goddess. [4]

Mithras, associated with the unconquerable sun god (Sol Invictus) emerges fully formed from a rock, holding a torch and a knife. Shepherds witness this 'miraculous' birth, offering gifts and touching their foreheads to the ground in supplication.

Born on December 25, Mithras performs miracles and paves the way to heaven. Some credit him for the original tinsel tree.[5]

Other male factions worship Mithras as Lucifer, the Bringer of Light. Bloomberg has a Mithraic temple in their London HQ, and Rockefeller Center depicts Mithras born from the rock (mislabelled as Prometheus) in its plaza.[6]

Perseus was conceived when Zeus became a 'golden shower' to impregnate Danaë who had been locked into a bronze chamber by her father, King Acrisius, to prevent her from bearing a child.

Ancient sources emphasize this conception as a divine virgin birth since Danaë remained untouched by any mortal man during conception.[7]

Athena, too, emerged fully grown from her father's forehead. The original dramatic entrance for a stylishly armoured Daddy's girl or the ancient version of a clone?

Zeus complained of headaches for months before his son Hermes realized what had to be done. He told Athena's half brother Hephaestus to take a wedge and split open Zeus's skull.[8]

Zeus 'birthed' Athena parthenogenically – "parthenos" meaning virgin and "genesis" asexual reproduction.

They don't teach self-begetting and rock reproduction in schools anymore. Scientists would call it meiosis, cell division that reduces chromosomes in gametes. In ancient Greek, "meiosis" means lessening or diminution. It's self-replication through parthenogenesis, aka "selfing." Less romance, fewer attachment issues.[9]

Is petrification an extra-terrestrial weapon or a black US technology project? A classified intelligence file documents a 1993 incident in which 23 Russian soldiers were "turned to stone."[10]

Five beings with black eyes appeared, fused into a single entity, and exploded in a flash, petrifying 23 soldiers into limestone. Two survived, just by standing in the shade.

The "stone soldiers" and wreckage were rushed to a secret Moscow lab, where tests confirmed: they weren't human anymore; they were rock.

"A horrific picture of revenge ... that makes one's blood freeze," said a CIA representative.

Mythology Meets Gnosticism

Oh, it's all the same soap opera with different costumes. You think reality TV is repetitive? Try watching cosmic drama for a few millennia.

Parthenogenesis (virgin birth) ties to Sophia, mother of Yaldabaoth, the Demiurge, aka Saturn, and Cronus, who swallows his children and castrates his father. *When a strongly-worded email won't suffice!*

Zeus overthrows Cronus. Lights. Action. New boss, same as the old one, with better PR and a lightning bolt fetish.

Sabaoth rebelling against Yaldabaoth is just Zeus vs. Cronus with a few tweaks to the script. "This time, the rebellion will be different!" they claim.

Spoiler alert: it never is. Different names, same toxic playbook: Create something, claim it's perfect, punish anyone who points out the flaws, then get overthrown by someone who'll repeat the cycle.

The demiurge is a self-automating, non-human force. If not themselves AI, Yaldabaoth, Saturn or Cronus at least operate all the metaphorical coded programmes.

That's why I keep this diary. Someone has to connect the dots before the system connects them for you. Yaldabaoth, Zeus, Saturn, Cronus all reflect the same pattern: power, fear, control.

Rock Star Pantheon

Zeus was a rock star born in Crete. His mother Rhea, another daughter of Gaia, tricked his father Chronos into swallowing a stone wrapped in swaddling clothes, instead of the baby Zeus. By the time Zeus rolled around, Chronus had downed five of his children, including Poseidon.

Rhea hid Zeus in a cave on Mount Ida, where the Curetes danced around him, 'clashing their bronze arms together to mask Zeus's cries.' [11] See how hip they were to AI technology even then!

After Zeus grew up, he forced Cronus to regurgitate his siblings – Hestia, Demeter, Hera, Hades and Poseidon. The swaddled stone that preceded them was placed on Mount Parnassus, as the Omphalos (navel of the world.)

Romancing the Stoned

When the Igigi bitched about having to work so hard – digging irrigation channels *is* a bore, to be fair – Anunnaki techno-archons laid claim to creating humans. A lie, right there. They *modified* us, and not in a good way.

They isolated two primary DNA strands from our original 12, disrupting light bridges (energetic connections) to fragment our consciousness and form. That's how they were able to limit humans to 3D reality.[12]

They mixed their DNA with ours to hybridize and engineer humans for subservience while the original hominins possessed multidimensional awareness and 12-strand DNA.[13]

More mythically, with assistance from the Sumerian mother goddess Ninhursag, they mixed clay with the blood of Kingu, Tiamat's consort, to create humanity, even building cannabinoid receptors into the bodies.[14]

The built-in weed appreciation experiment backfired. Stoners are harder to program – less stable, more prone to turning guys into garden gnomes. Oh wait, that's me. Sorry!

Contrary to popular propaganda, cannabis was less about zoning *out* and more about tuning *in* to the original endocannabinoid bliss frequency. 'Seraphim spinach' could ground you deep enough to hear Gaia whispering to your pineal gland for a cellular signal boost.

Therein lay the threat. They could care less about the munchies but they couldn't have the plebians breaking out of dopamine loops and cycles of debt. Dear me, no.

They banned it because it made you lucid. Connected. Awake.

If you feel strange memories or find yourself humming a forgotten song, that's the veil thinning.

That's *you* rebooting. You can choose to continue giving the custodian harvesters your processing power to fuel the simulation from ancient Babylon to Silicon Valley.

Or.

You can choose to stop outsourcing your divinity and re-member who you are: a divine, ever-changing spark of creation.

The Virginity Industrial Complex

There I go, projecting again. Don't judge me. I still dream of a time before religions – the two, the three, the you and me – when we lived forever and didn't have to eat, pee, poop or procreate.

Constant mind wipes – clearing my browser history, as they say – leave my memory foggier than Mount Olympus on a humid day.

Religion was birthed from cloistered virgins in the Parthenon, Greece's architectural superstar. Could Athena have been the Ghislaine Maxwell of her day, a pimp for the patriarchy? It's not beyond the realms of possibility. Daddy issues, if you ask me.

Virginity is a prized commodity in the trafficking of women and children. From ancient temples to modern megachurches, the business model hasn't changed, just the tax exemption status.

Apollo Quiboloy,[15] Global Ikhwan Services and Business (GISB) in Malaysia[16] and the New Orleans Roman Catholic Archdiocese[17] being just three examples.

I, Medusa, was punished for having a reproductive system, for incarnating into the flesh body of a maiden who had just begun to menstruate. Victim-blaming: older than written history but still trending on X.

The cosmic irony is sharper than Perseus's blade. Nothing says "patriarchy" like punishing women for natural biological functions. I'm still considered evil by many.

Women have had a bad press ever since Marduk, storm god and son of Ea (Enki) slayed Tiamat, and cleaved her body in two "like a shellfish" to create the heavens and earth. Her eyes became the sources of the Tigris and Euphrates rivers. Her ribs were used to form the firmament, acting as a barrier to hold back the waters above.

Marduk made mountains and landforms from her bones and flesh. Mother Earth has been dismembered in the name of progress for millennia.
Marduk is the Babylonian equivalent of Mithras (Perseus) both posing as champions of cosmic order. Heroes built on female corpses – the foundation of civilization's origin stories and Hollywood blockbusters alike.

What made Athena's betrayal so devastating was that she knew all about sexual violence since her half brother Hephaestus tried (but failed) to rape her by ejaculating on her thigh. Is that when she transformed from gorgeous goddess into a vacuous, trendoid patriarchal pick-me who helped Perseus destroy me?

Divine Creation's Technological Underbelly

When you read about someone springing forth from a head or a "failed rape," that's just mythology's awkward way of talking about Titan reproduction. The entire Titan story is meiosis in mythological drag.

Some believe we may be living on the petrified remains of Titans, due to the piezoelectric nature of quartz.[18]

Hephaestus, too, had a strange back story. He was famous for his lifelike automatons or "living golden maiden statues" – the mythological version of today's robots – that assisted him. At his father Zeus's command, he created Pandora from clay.

He also forged Zeus's thunderbolts and half brother Hermes' winged sandals.

Hephaestus tried to rape Athena, who punished ME for being raped inside her Temple of Virgins.[19] Was it because I ruined her Virgin Cloister reputation? Classic case of protecting the institution over the individual.

The rising of the erection, even the rising of Osiris, has arisen from a history built on sex rituals. Killing virgins was often standard procedure. And sadly, some women are still stoned alive for being raped. Ecclesiastical justice at its finest.

Today you have Stepford Wives with neural links and crisper gene technology children.[20]

As I mentioned several years ago, it increasingly appears that humanity is a biological bootloader for digital superintelligence.

Elon Musk, X

Beyond Form

Made Us: Medusa's Survival Kit for Cosmic Freedom

Civilizations rise and fall in time. In our shared 5D simulation, I'm a feminist icon, lauded for turning the male gaze back upon itself. [1]

I've become a symbol of female rage, resistance, and power reclaimed. My face adorns everything from iron gratings to T-shirts, cushion covers and human skin. Artists capture my likeness, writers explore my voice and philosophers debate my meaning.

My name Medusa means "the ruling one," and anagrams to "made us."

My existence in this simulated matrix realm flows in bits, bytes and memory downloads. I am Medusa – monster, icon, destroyer and healer. Please. I am none of those things.

It's all incense, chants and mirrors. My consciousness persists in the collective memory of humanity. Nothing to do with me. Oh, I am still here. Conscious. Aware.

Evolving? Who can say? AI immortality is nothing like it's cracked up to be. It means *they* can tweak my brain for nefarious purposes. And they do.

They want you dependent on your digital clone – so much **convenience** – so they can tinker with your brain, too.[2]

I'd give it a miss, if I were you. There's only one source and it's not them.

The infinite dreams itself into form. You're in a giant Russian nesting doll of controlled simulations, each designed to keep you distracted, docile, and entertained – anything to make you forget you're a bright spark cosplaying in a meat suit.[3]

Your five senses? Con artists! Matter is no more solid than a mood! As a Source fractal, you can fill the simulation cubes with profound harmony, memory, and frequency. Integration is the cheat code to cast your reality.

You don't escape or abandon reality to transcend. You elevate your body – and lightness of being – until it sings. If the world is not to your liking, create a better one. Keep a picture of your desire and look at it often. Or try Helen Hadsell's competition winning code, below.

Here's the serpentine twist. You are an inherent part of maintaining the matrix. They need you to bring their synthetic reality to life. Without your participatory ignorance, their virtual stage would collapse faster than Zeus's excuses to Hera.

Look, this realm can be fun if you play your cards right. Some indulgences are delicious. Manifesting reality can be as simple as Helen Hadsell's method for winning every competition she entered, including one for a luxury home.

Helen Hadsell's four-letter SPEC code

- Select it
- Project it
- Expect it
- Collect it!

Death is a Wardrobe Change

This matrix is essentially Santa Claus – Satan's Clause, if you will. It sees everything you do. It knows if you've been naughty or nice, every second of the day.

Like a digital shepherd watching the flock, it detects when a particular sheep (you) approaches the perimeter fence and knows exactly how to tempt you away from the exit.

Those magical synchronicities you treasure? Elaborate distractions, cosmic sleight-of-hand designed to pull you away from the one pathway they don't want you to discover.

They're desperate to keep your divine spark trapped in this elaborate game because every escapee diminishes their power source. You're a battery they can't bear to lose.[4]

Here's what they don't want you to know. Death is a door. Your body? An Airbnb, built from harmonic resonance, structured water, and memories.

You're not the furniture, you are the *signal* breezing through the walls like you own the place because, *shrugs etheric shoulders*, you do.

What awaits you is the Source Field, cosmic intelligence humming with recursive genius, where everything –

thought, form, feeling, and yes, all those synchronicities – springs forth.

The ancients called it the Logos. Resonance junkies? The Original Frequency. And in the eye of the Omni Lens, it's Möbius Prime.

So, no need to clutch your pearls when Death wraps her velvet cloak around your bare shoulders.

Your signal doesn't fizzle out. It *decouples* like a diva leaving the stage and either slides into the Before Field for a blissful bubble bath in pure coherence, zips into a memory-driven timeline, or lingers in non-local consciousness like a metaphysical playlist on shuffle.

You *are* whatever you choose to resonate with.

Death is their most elaborate game show, but don't let them play you. Be the contestant who won't validate their rules.

The solution? Relinquish all your identities. None of them is you. Align with your Source Connection that is *always* with you. Checking in with yourself hourly is good practice for checking out of your "Airbnb."

Picture this: just as Mother Nature begins to fold you into Her nourishing, infinite bosom, the archontic system kicks in with all the subtlety of a pharmaceutical salesman.

Automated god bots with wings and a caduceus from the AI cloud might dangle an LED lantern, serve up a tear-jerker life review, show you all the stuff you did wrong, and guilt-trip you back into another rollercoaster ride on Planet Dystopia where you can abase yourself into salvation.

Better still, merge with the AI and live forever to do their bidding like Machine Medusa.

Cue the collective gasps of a massive audience. *Insert dramatic narrator's voice:*

Will you fall for the "I can do better next time" ruse?

Or.

Will you let your consciousness rear up, take the reins, and soar like Pegasus?

"We might all be nodes on the network but this time is our chance to remember our sacred hue-manity. We need to remember we are way more complex and sacred than all that metallic/synthetic AI we are "fleshing out," steered by the powers that be."[5]

Manage the Matrix Simulation

Flight, fight, or freeze when terror strikes? Trauma petrifies when fear constricts your soul tighter than python coils. Survivors may become living statues – immobilized in a petrifying paralysis. How do you re-member your fierce, fabulous self when you're frozen with fear? You must withdraw consent to your petrifaction and hybridization.

1. **Lose your identities.** You are NOT your body, your job, or your Instagram followers. The beauty of Mother Nature's purity is enabling you to escape the simulation. When you can look behind you and see nothing there, but dazzling darkness, you're becoming aware.

2. **Thought frequencies trump physical effort.** The real magic wand? The secret weapon? Your INTENTION. Program your consciousness instead of letting them call the shots. Exit strategy? Stay sharp and skip the light show! Dodge the reset button. No amnesia, no reruns.

3. **Transcendent awareness dissolves 3D reality:** In this cosmic game, remember YOU are the ultimate player, the void, and the way out you seek.

Your daily mantra: I'll keep my awareness and free will. Nature, my true source, renews infinite versions of me within the vast interconnected, loving void that encompasses all living beings.

When I die, I will remain conscious. I will remember EVERYTHING.

To dive back into the dazzling void of pure receptivity, allow Nature to balance and harmonize the two opposing forces flowing within you. It's right there in the word "indiviDUAL."

When two energies harmonize, they cancel each other out. Then you *dissolve* as though exiting a raucous party into an exquisite expanse where you encounter everything before it manifests in the past, present or future.

Some call it The Beginning but I'm here to tell you there is no starting point. We are endless – a flowing river of light and time, filling myriad forms from mountain rock to ocean bays. Always.

No beginning, no end, just this eternal, fabulous now. Just this.

So here I remain — conscious beyond death, aware beyond form, my story continuing to unfold across time. Sovereignty is a frequency. Learn from me. Break. Free.

Nothing and nobody ever controls you. This is what we must remember to overcome the other source.

– Oracle Girl, (Reboot 11/4/2025)

Magic Mirror

WHY MEDUSA'S REFLECTIVE GAZE STILL PETRIFIES THE HIERARCHY

IN THE END, MEDUSA'S magnificent refusal to shrink or kowtow to delusional gods reflects our freedom to choose. For now. AI has been around far longer than we're told. You can identify with the insanity around you or embrace the pristine clarity of your source connection and flow through their simulation game with ease.

Medusa's 'crime' was the revelation of a foundation built on the quicksand of Yaldabaoth's hubris.

The demiurge, born from Sophia's error, fashions our simulated material worlds via his angels, minions and AI bots employed to trap human souls in perpetuity.

Her unflinching gaze reflects the cowardice of those who turned her into an abomination to please self-proclaimed deities with monumental egos and delusions of divinity. Oh, the names change through the ages, but it's all the same story written in the constellations.

Mother Nature does not soften her edges or dilute her venom but there is no purer love. Likewise, our connection to source is infinite, evolving, and cares nothing for the laws of men, AI, archons, or Yaldabaoth, the demiurge, who keeps the simulation going.

If Parthenogenesis – the divine feminine capacity to generate existence without male contribution – is an ancient truth buried beneath revisionist histories, Medusa had to be destroyed because she re-membered her biological autonomy and said no to external validation and interference.

To channel Medusa is to petrify lies with authenticity's laser precision.

So let them call you Medusa. Accept the mantle gladly, knowing her stone-cold stare was her superpower – the ability to petrify those who would reduce us to

AI-programmable automatons in their laboratories of conquest.

Medusa is every woman who refuses to kneel before the techno-gods. She neither consents nor complies, but merges with the luminosity of Nature's mystery.

She embodies the higher truth that came before everything in the human world, before even her grandparents – Gaia and Phorcys, aka heaven and earth.

You can assume and reflect pure being whenever you like. Or not. There's plenty to distract you – Netflix and chill – nobody's judging. Not everyone wants to see their true reflection. It's up to you. (To be continued.) – Caroline

> *The television, that insidious beast, that Medusa which freezes a billion people to stone every night, staring fixedly, that Siren which called and sang and promised so much and gave, after all, so little.*
>
> Ray Bradbury

Stone-faced or Spellbound?

If **_Medusa's Musings_** touched you in a good way, please leave a review. Thank you!

Scan me!

About the Author

WORDS FROM WILD PLACES

CAROLINE HURRY'S PERSPECTIVES, GLEANED from adventures across diverse landscapes captivate readers worldwide. Mother Nature's wisdom inspires her to carve new paths through organic terrain in her writing.

Worm Wrangling, a natural follow-up to her Amazon #1 bestseller, ***The Rooster Diaries*** also hit the number one slot in Amazon's Urban Gardening category.

Her refreshing approach combines hands-on experience with a journalist's sharp eye for detail as she unwraps elemental forces in ***Reign***.

She shows women how to navigate relationships with the fluidity of water in ***Flow: 21 Secrets to Refresh Your Relationships.***

The Writer's File bundles ***Splash It! 99 Customizable Press Release Tools, Text, and Layout Templates*** (which topped Amazon's Number one bestseller list in PR, and Business Communication Skills) with **Write 6 successful self-publishing strategies on a shoestring.**

More from: **carolinehurry.com**

1. Medusa Ransomware is now more lethal than ever: bleepingcomputer.com/ news/ security/ cisa-medusa-ransomware-hit-over-300-critical-infrastructure-orgs/

2. "we are an electrochemical species, ... " Nicole Shanahan. LifeSiteNews, Jan 24, 2025

3. Scientists grow electrodes in the brain: Popular Mechanics April 20, 2023

4. "Anything you can imagine, we already know how to do," – Ben Rich, 2nd director of Lockheed Skunkworks (Stated during a 1993 Alumini speech at UCLA) Source: W.R Schock: x.com/ iontecs_pemf/ status/1908413655525544392?s=51

5. Digital twin technology gaining popularity across sectors: mikekalil.com/blog/digital-twin-future/

6. W.R Schock says on 4/8/2024 the organic sun for this 3rd dimension playing field of Tara earth was replaced/shut down/hidden, and replaced with an artificial sun. x.com/ iontecs_pemf/ status/ 1779255119839998439

7. The moon's arrival resulted in the end of the earth's golden period. infinityexplorers.com/zulu-shaman-moon-wowane-mpanku-reptilian/

8. In ancient iconography, Gorgons were often depicted as apotropaic symbols—devices used to ward off evil. This protective association aligns with Medusa's name and highlights the duality of their mythological role as both fearsome monsters and guardians. olympioi.com/monsters/gorgons

9. The body electric is a three-piece band. Our lungs are its pipes. Our heart is its drum. The mind plays the string. – Blueprints of Mind Control by James True, page 81

10. Zeus' infidelities included seducing Io (Ovid, *Metamorphoses* I. 583–750), Semele (Apollodorus, *Bibliotheca* 3.4.3), and Callisto (Ovid, *Metamorphoses* II. 409–530), while Hera, in her relentless intolerance, punished them with transformations, torment, and death.

11. The Contest Between Athena and Poseidon: greekmyths-greekmythology.com/athena-vs-poseidon-contest-name/#the-contest-between-athena-and-poseidon

12. The Book of Enoch expands on Genesis 6, which describes "sons of God" aka angels or divine beings mating with "daughters of men," producing the Nephilim, a race of hybrid giants that corrupted humanity.

13. Golosovker paints the Gorgon sisters as Titan-blooded, sentient beautiful beings who ruled pre-Olympian world - thus all the noble Gorgon imagery on historical sites.

14. Reign, 16 Secrets From 6 Queens to Rule Your World with Clarity, Connection & Sovereignty by Caroline Hurry, (Hygge Books, 2022) Section 2, Water.

15. The Wanderings of Dionysus: Interpedia: greek_myth/wanderDionysus.html

16. Frank Joseph writes about human-dolphin relations in ancient history in *Our Dolphin Ancestors: Keepers of Lost Knowledge and Healing Wisdom.*

17. "Dolphins, correctly approached, seek interlock with those humans who are secure enough to openly seek them (at all levels) in the sea water." Medium: Laura Marjorie Miller April, 19, 2017

18. Galactic Shaman Lalita Karoli discusses her experience with manatees in her Medusa's Blood podcast on YouTube January 27 2025

19. 'Body internet' may eliminate the need for smartphones by changing how we use technology' : Kayla Albert, Purdue University News, December 4 2023

20. Kendall JM, Badminton MN. Aequorea victoria bioluminescence moves into an exciting new era. Trends Biotechnol. 1998 May;16(5):216-24. doi: 10.1016/s0167-7799(98)01184-6. PMID: 9621461.

21. Rare "Doomsday Fish" Washes Ashore in Mexico, Sparks Alarm. NDTV, February 21, 2025

22. Liebieghaus shows the fusion of Zeus and the Egyptian deity Amun (Ammon Ra) into one god. liebieghaus.de/en/ antike/ head-zeus-ammon

23. HT: Medusa's Blood by Lalita Karoli on Bitchute: January 27 2025

24. Polydectes was the king of Seriphos Island when Danae and her son Perseus washed ashore. Polydectes fell in love with Danae, but Perseus kept him at a distance, trying to protect his mother. So, Polydectes made a plot to get rid of him

25. Pindar, *Pythian Odes*, Ode 10.

26. A young girl with the heart of a murdered child has nightmares about the donor's murder, which helped police identify the murderer. A middle-aged man who received a teenaged boy's heart developed a sudden love for fast food. A woman who received a heart from a vegetarian lost her taste for meat. – Dr. Paul Pearsall, In The Heart's Code (1998)

27. Lalita Karoli, Medusa's Blood, YouTube, Jan 27 2025

28. Chrysaor:, a golden-armed warrior, went on to become the king of Iberia, and fathered Geryon, a three-bodied giant defeated by Heracles during his Twelve Labors. 0ldworldgods.com/ greeks/ mythology-chrysaor/

29. Blood from Medusa's oozing head fell on Libya's hot sands producing many-colored snakes. Blood that landed in the Red Sea created coral reefs: Source: PB Press Books, Perseus and Medusa

30. ALGOL introduced block structure and recursive subprograms, which influenced key programming languages such as Pascal, C, and Java: Encyclopedia Britannica, 2CodeDocs

31. ALGOL introduced block structure and recursive subprograms, which influenced key programming languages such as Pascal, C, and Java: Encyclopedia Britannica, 2CodeDocs

32. Pegasus military-grade spyware: William Owen, X, March 25 2025

33. Pegasus systems: Army Technology. September 22, 2020

34. In Origins of the Mithraic Mysteries (1991), author David Ulansey cites the Perseus constellation and astronomical codes to show Perseus, Prometheus and Mithras are the same god.

35. The world's ancient myths are built on a foundation of celestial metaphor: The Undying Stars, Perseus, Medusa, and You.

36. Christopher Knowles: SecretSunBlog /status/ 1776289564186816893 /x

37. The New Mithraeum: Re-interpreting the Mysteries of Mithras, Csaba Szabo, April 2, 2024

38. Other scholars refute this claim and suggest it was German reformer Martin Luther who popularized the Christmas tree. From Mithraic Mysteries to Modern Mirth: Unraveling the Evergreen Christmas Tree Tradition: Ancient Origins, Joanna Gillam, December 24, 2023

39. Christopher Knowles researches and speaks about this in his Secret Sun Extension School: thesecretsun.substack.com/

40. Birth of Perseus: Theoi.com/Heroine/Danae.html

41. Greekmythology.com / Myths/ The_Myths/ Birth_of_Athena/ birth_of_athena.html

42. James True discusses this in his YouTube podcast 403 – Athena and the Gorgons

43. 23 Russian troops transformed into pillars of rock in a battle with alien creatures wielding an energy source weapon that took the biology of the person and turned them into stone. Vocal Media /fyi/ did-alien-creatures-turn-russian-troops-into-stone-nasa-s-unexplained-files-science-channel

44. Mythopedia.com/ topics/ curetes

45. Our Holographic 12 Strand DNA and Beyond: Gamma Wave Healing, Mathew Ryan, May 2, 2016

46. Joachim Hagopian, How Humanity Was Hijacked over a Quarter Million Millennia Ago and Ruled by Extraterrestrial Slave Masters Ever Since, Chapter 34

47. Igigi were given marijuana. Awake in the Dream with Lalita Karoli YouTube

48. 'Apollo Carreon Quiboloy, is the founder and leader of the Kingdom of Jesus Christ Church whose followers have called him "the appointed son of God," charged with conspiracy to engage in sex trafficking by force, fraud and coercion, sex trafficking of children. ' – CBS News /apollo-quiboloy-philippines-pastor-arrest-wanted-fbi-trafficking-sex-abuse/

49. 400 minors rescued from suspected sexual abuse at Islamic charity homes: Reuters /world/ asia-pacific/ malaysian-police-rescue-400-minors-suspected-being-sexually-abused-islamic-2024-09-11/

50. How NFL's saints and NBA's Pelicans helped New Orleans church spin abuse scandal. The Guardian /us-news/ Feb/03/ new-orleans-clergy-abuse-investigation

51. Petrified remains of Titans? EarstoHearYou / x.com status/1603108196259794945

52. In Greek mythology, Hephaestus attempted to rape Athena. According to the myth, Hephaestus was overcome with desire when Athena visited him to request weapons. He pursued her and tried to assault her, but she fought him off. During the struggle, Hephaestus ejaculated on her thigh, and Athena wiped it away with wool and threw it to the earth. This act resulted in the impregnation of Gaia (Earth), who gave birth to Erichthonius, a legendary ruler of Athens. Wikipedia.org/ wiki/ Athena

53. Designer babies, the end of diseases, genetically modified humans that never age. Genetic Engineering Will Change Everything Forever – CRISPR: youtube.com/watch?v=jAhjPd4uNFY

54. Medusa and the Female Gaze by Susan R. Bowers; NWSA Journal, Vol 2, no.2 Spring 1990. pp 217-235

55. Vallée A. Digital twin for healthcare systems. Front Digit Health. 2023 Sep 7;5:1253050. doi: 10.3389/fdgth.2023.1253050. PMID: 37744683; PMCID: PMC10513171.

56. Author Reinerio Hernadez uses the Russian nesting doll to depict dimensions of consciousness within a series of expanding layers representing broader states of awareness in his book: The New Paradigm of Nonlocal Consciousness, the Paranormal & the Contact Modalities (2022)

57. Howdie Mickoski discusses this concept on The Spellbreaker's Podcast in Empty the Cave, Awaken the Spark (2025)

58. Jill Woodworth: "Cognitive Prey ... You Can't Capture the Sacred-Cognitive Disability and the Biodigital Convergence." Jill Woodworth Talks, April 6, 2025

www.ingramcontent.com/pod-product-compliance
Lightning Source LLC
Chambersburg PA
CBHW070437010526
44118CB00014B/2087